Soa

M
MW01504621

Contents

What's Happening?

Where did the water go?

Where did the water go?

Where did the milk go?

Where did the suntan lotion go?

The water that
was <u>on</u> the plate
is now <u>in</u>
the towel.

The water that
was <u>on</u> the soil
is now <u>in</u>
the soil.

The milk that was <u>on</u> the floor is now <u>in</u> the sponge.

The suntan lotion that was <u>on</u> the skin is now <u>in</u> the skin.

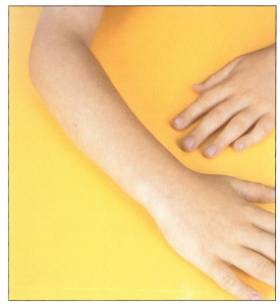

Absorb means to soak up a liquid with a solid.

The towel
absorbs
the water.

The soil
absorbs
the water.

The sponge
absorbs
the milk.

The skin
absorbs
the suntan
lotion.

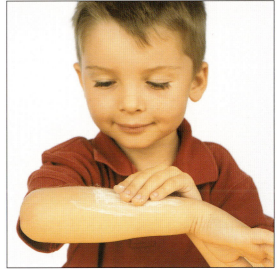

Try this experiment.

What you need

1 paper towel

4 small bowls

water

4 colors of food coloring

a spoon

What you do

1. Fold the paper towel in half and then in half again.

2. Pour some water into each bowl.

3. Put about 8 drops of food coloring into each bowl.

4. Stir the water in each bowl.

5. Dip one corner of the paper towel into the first bowl of colored water.

6. Dip another corner of the paper towel into the second bowl.

7. Dip the third corner of the paper towel into the third bowl.

8. Dip the fourth corner of the paper towel into the fourth bowl.

9. Unfold the paper towel.

The colored water was absorbed into the paper towel.

Which Materials Absorb?

Try this experiment.

What you need

6 aluminum pie plates

water

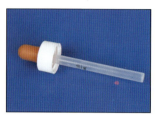
a dropper

Testing Materials

a sponge

wax paper

a paper plate

newspaper

a cloth

plastic wrap

What you do

1. Place one of the testing materials in each pie plate.

2. Squeeze 4 drops of water onto each material. Observe what happens.

3. Record your observations in a chart like this.

	Does Absorb	Does Not Absorb
sponge		
wax paper		
paper plate		
newspaper		
cloth		
plastic wrap		

The Clean-Up Challenge

Martin, Becky, and Randy all accidentally spilled their milk.

Martin is going to
use a sponge
to clean it up.

Becky is going to
use a paper towel
to clean it up.

Randy is going to
use plastic wrap
to clean it up.

Who will clean up the spilled milk the fastest?

Something to Think About

It's good that some things absorb.

It's good that some things don't absorb.

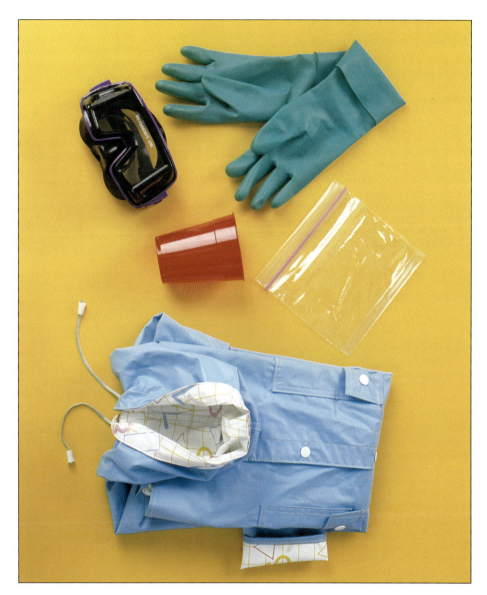

Make an Invisible Design

What you need

a piece of paper   cooking oil   a small paintbrush

a large paintbrush   watercolor paints

What you do

1. With the small paintbrush, use the oil to paint a picture on the paper.

2. Use the large paintbrush to cover the whole paper with paint.

What happens when you paint over the oil?

Questions

1. What does **absorb** mean?
2. What are three materials that absorb?
3. What are three materials that do not absorb?
4. When would you want to have materials that absorb?